# The Little Duck

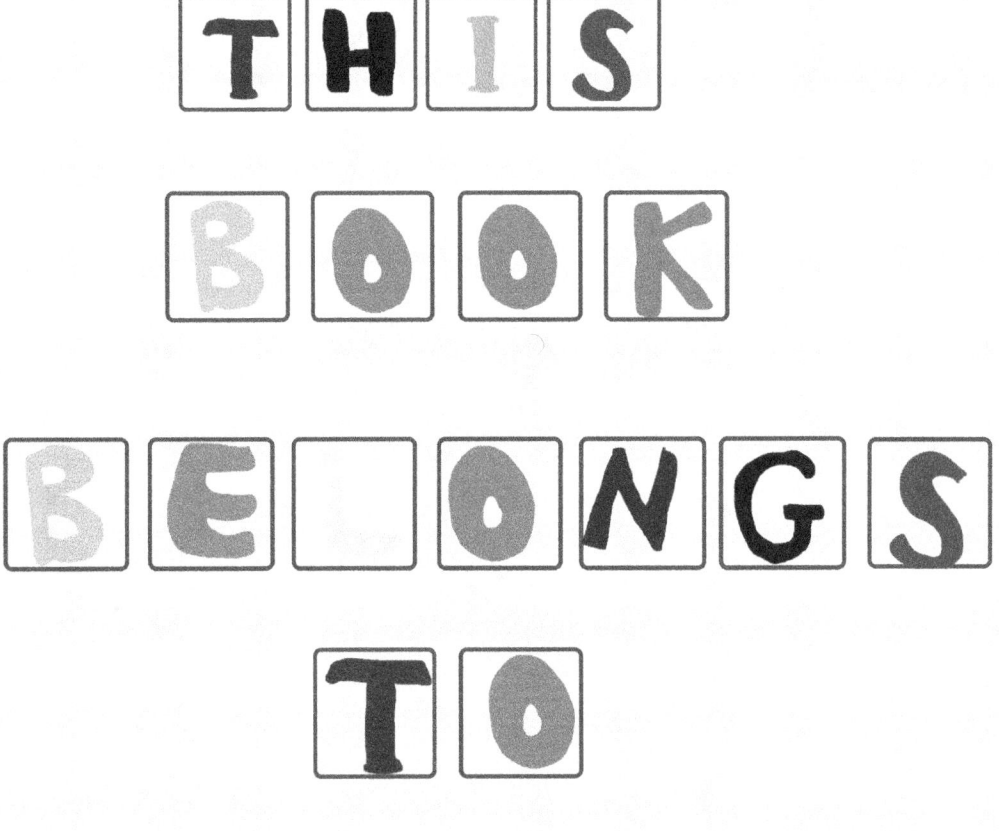

THIS BOOK BELONGS TO

........................

# The little duck lives in a farm with her friends

# The little duck loves to learn numbers

# The little duck stopped and said

# 1
# One tree

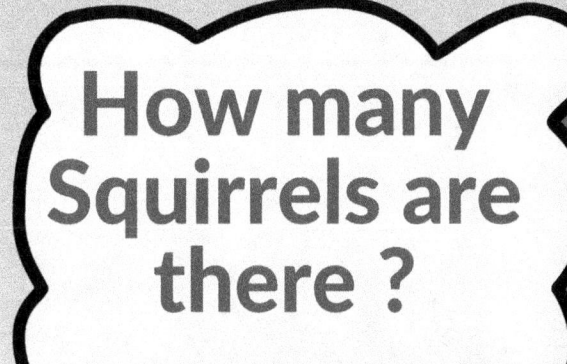

# 2
# Two squirrels

# 3
# Three bees

# 4
# Four stars

# 5

# Five balls

# 6
# Six sheep

# 7
# Seven pumpkins

# 8
# Eight apple trees

# 9
# Nine watermelons

# 10
# Ten Balloons

www.ingramcontent.com/pod-product-compliance
Lightning Source LLC
LaVergne TN
LVHW060133080526
838201LV00118B/3042